MEETING THE AUTHENTIC YOU!

MEETING THE AUTHENTIC YOU!

CONVERSATIONS WITH WHITNEY & DWAYNE

Whitney D. Smith & Dwayne Graham

The opinions expressed in this manuscript are solely the opinions of the author and do not represent the opinions or thoughts of the publisher. The author has represented and warranted full ownership and/or legal right to publish all the materials in this book.

Meeting The Authentic You
Conversations with Whitney & Dwayne
All Rights Reserved.
Copyright © 2016 Whitney Smith and Dwayne Graham
v1.0

Cover Design by: Richard McDonald, Just Rich Designs. All rights reserved - used with permission.

Editor: LesLie Patterson.

This book may not be reproduced, transmitted, or stored in whole or in part by any means, including graphic, electronic, or mechanical without the express written consent of the publisher except in the case of brief quotations embodied in critical articles and reviews.

Outskirts Press, Inc.
http://www.outskirtspress.com

ISBN: 978-1-4787-7461-7

Outskirts Press and the "OP" logo are trademarks belonging to Outskirts Press, Inc.

PRINTED IN THE UNITED STATES OF AMERICA

This book is dedicated to...
All the people who are tired of being less than God's Best!

Whitney: Avery V. Turton-you are the reason I live and dream!
Dwayne: To my Parents and my inspiration (my son).

Acknowledgments

*Thank you to those who invested in us
and supported us along the way.
We love you!*

Table of Contents

"If I Would Have Gotten My Way I Wouldn't
Be the Woman I Am Today!" 1
Mutual Attraction, Different Perspectives 4
Embrace Your Singleness 6
Women of Strength 9
The Chains Have Been Broken (Part 1) 11
I Refuse! (Part 1) 12
The Chains Have Been Broken (Part 2) 13
Bumped Back to Start! "SORRY!" 15
I Have A Dream… 17
You Are Still Here! 19
Suppressing the Pains and Living with the Memories 21
Where Do Broken Hearts Go? 22
The Familiar vs. The Unfamiliar (Part 1) 24
Stop Picking at Your Wounds! Let the Scabs Heal! 25
I Didn't Know I Needed HEALING! 28
I Am God's Masterpiece! 30
Haven't You Had Enough? 32
Your Reality vs. Their Perception 34
The Familiar vs. The Unfamiliar! (Part 2) 36
What Is the Last Thing God Said to YOU? (Part 1) 38
People Think They Know, but They Have No Clue! 41

Learning How to Live with the Judgment 44
What Was the Last Thing God Said to YOU? (Part 2) 46
Pause…Hit the Reset Button. 48
"What Is It About Them Doors?" (Part 1) 50
One of Six 51
When Being Vulnerable and Exposed Hurts! 53
"What Is It About Them Doors?" (Part 2) 55
Speak Life! (Part 1) 57
How So You Benefit by Being in Competition with Me? 59
Speak Life! (Part 2) 61
Breaking Boxing Match News: Me vs. Myself! 62
Whitney D. Smith 67
Dwayne Graham 69

The Impetus for the INSPIRATION

Whitney and I came together one day to discuss the possibilities of penning an open letter to women, a women's meditational book.

We discussed in depth some of the issues and challenges women were encountering and decided to jot down inspirational and empowering messages to propel women to begin seeing themselves from a different perspective, a new lens, new vision: seeing ourselves as healthy, happy, and spiritual beings.

What inspired this Book?
The anger many women live with!
The shame many women live with!
The disappointment many women live with!
The bitterness many women live with!
The hopelessness many women live with!
The fear many women live with!

The purpose of this Book?
To inspire Women to See themselves
from a Healthier and Empowered perspective!
To inspire Women to Envision more for themselves.
Leaving the past pain and hurts.
To inspire Women to Dream again!
To Inspire Women to Aim Higher!
To Inspire Women to Let Go of what hurts!
To Inspire Women to Heal where we once Hurt and Love Again!

Our Hope is these inspiring and empowering messages would provide clarity where confusion reigns, Replace pain for a Peace surpassing all understanding, Acceptance where anger abounds, Healing where we harbored hurt, Truth where Self-deception tread, and a New Vision of Self.

This is the Great Exchange between God and Us, old things are passed away, and we are created anew in Him.

This song "The Great Exchange" by Martha Munizzi speaks to the exchange, which occurs between believer and God.

His joy my strength,
His grace my peace My fear erased my heart is free
His joy my strength,
His grace my peace My sin erased my heart is free
His joy my strength,
His grace my peace My fear erased my heart is free

This is the great exchange,
I'm trading my sorrows for the garment of Praise
Heaven is open every time I praise,
This is the great, this is the great exchange

Yeah beauty for ashes and joy for my pain,
He turns weeping into dancing every time I praise
Burdens are lifting doubts begin to cease,
Removes the heavy the burdens and brings the sweetest peace

This is the great exchange,
I'm trading my sorrows for the garment of Praise
Heaven is open every time I praise,
This is the great, this is the great exchange

My fear he is taking replacing with dancing and singing a song of deliverance
His joy my strength,
His grace my peace My fear erased my heart is free

Forward

By Rai Camille Rance

We pray these reflections and insights are mere glimpses of what's to come. Get ready! Your prelude to purpose is preparation for God's promise to you. With each step and misstep along your journey this collection of meditations is designed with you in mind! The Creator has NOT forgotten you. We encourage you to live RIGHT now! Don't wait. Why wait? You have a Divine Partner in this. Seeking His "guidance" (God Dancing with You >>Letting Him take the Lead) at every turn and dip. Speak Life at home, at work, in your car, at the gym, over your child, for your family, your finances, your spouse, and for your future God ordained & designed life mate. He's Intentional. You be Intentional! Every encounter shall increase my faith. STOP!! Take a moment (don't stay there) look where He's "brought you from." His resume is Spotless!! If He did it before He can and will do it again! In Him we are a new creation, daily renewal with Him and in Him, pressing toward (ahead) the mark of this HIGHER calling.

"If I Would Have Gotten My Way I Wouldn't Be the Woman I Am Today!"

He was one of my best friends for 5 years prior to us dating. During our friendship we grew closer and began to develop strong feelings for one another. We both mutually agreed to take our relationship/friendship to the next level. As time passed, slowly, I became more and more frustrated. My expectations of our "relationship" were not being met. I felt something was missing and I deserved "more." We dated exclusively for 3 years; however, our "relationship" was a closely regarding secret. When we went out I was introduced as a "friend", yet my family and best friends all knew we were "together."

What frustrated me most?

Our (my) relationship was hidden, I was a secret; I questioned myself and my decision to wait 3 ½ years for a committed relationship and the title of being "his lady."

The last few years of our relationship, these issues (my issue) became increasingly challenging. My issue became a thorn in my side. I couldn't go to the altar with the man I loved (as a couple). In private we exchanged all the benefits of coupledom, in public, we were just friends, and mere acquaintances. We traveled to weddings and events. I pretended I didn't love him; However, I wanted everyone, including his family, to know we were a couple. I wanted him to want the same things I wanted from this relationship! He would regularly tell me to be patient, as he waited on God to give him and answer regarding our "relationship." Or he'd say, "it's not you it's me." I listened, I wanted to believe what he said, and what we shared was real. I believed that things would soon turn around. I waited, I was impatient, and I was anxious, and carrying frustration (Reference Philippians 4:6).

I'd ask myself why I was waiting. My family and friends asked the same questions of me, asking why are you settling? Why are you compromising when you deserve so much more than you are receiving? Eventually, after 3 ½ years, I made the decision to move forward and begin living the life God planned for me. This was and has not been an easy task. There were times I could not resist the temptation to see him one more time. Finally, I realized this load was too heavy a burden to bare alone (Reference Matthew 11:30). I asked God for strength to carry this and help me move on.

My best girlfriends were my source of strength. I confided in them and expressed my disappointment in wasting so much time waiting for a commitment and why it took me so long to understand I was not a secret to be hidden, but a princess becoming a queen, a gem, a pearl, and a diamond in the rough.

I now had lots of time to reflect on my experiences. These revelations opened my eyes and I viewed life with a different perspective. I didn't notice God working on me throughout my previous "relationship." I was distracted and fixated on what "I" wasn't getting. I had not considered the ways in which God was developing me, preparing me, and refining me. My relationship taught me (forced me) to become a better communicator, I was no longer impulsive, and I was developing patience. God used my relationship to get my attention. God wanted my undivided attention. When I got to the place where my back was against a wall... I was in a perfect position for God to use me, change me, and increase my faith in Him. My relationship was not a "waste of time." I've learned valuable lessons. What the enemy may have meant for my harm, God used my situation for my good. It was not a waste of time (Reference Genesis 50:20)!

Ladies Reflection

Consider your last relationship. For those of you currently in a committed relationship, consider what's not going your way. Reflect back mentally utilizing emotional visitation to accomplish the deep reflection and self-awareness. I'm suggesting…

Are you better or bitter since your breakup? What were the catalyst and or shift from like to love? Did you break up or consider breaking up to become a better you? If yes, why?

Mutual Attraction, Different Perspectives

Men are most captivated by the physical beauty and features that women possess—their smile, eyes, lips, hips, breasts, booty, and of course the way they dress! In most cases these are the same reasons women are attracted to men. You gals are attracted to our smile, smell, body, height, and style of dress.

The mutual attraction, in most cases, is a matter of physical attraction. The physical/mutual attraction becomes a set-up for a verbal dialogue in which ideals and perspectives are exchanged. When an intimate moment of honesty and vulnerability transpires during a conversation between two people who share a mutual attraction, there may be an opportunity to experience something that will be life changing or life enhancing!

Initially, women and men enter into each other's lives with unchallenged physical attraction, which later becomes mutual. But once perspectives are exchanged, here come the challenges! As a man, I've met women whom I've been very physically attracted to and who were physically attracted to me; however, for the most part, the attraction remained physical because we differed in our perspectives as they pertained to how we individually envisioned our lives regarding relationships, commitment, and marriage.

While many women and a select few men desire to be involved in committed relationships, there are a growing number of men and women who are more focused on pursuing their dreams and becoming more established in life rather than committing to relationships and getting married! The other perspective is that there are also a growing number of men and women who shun the thought of or hope for commitment and marriage because of their own personal experiences or the horrific experiences of others.

Countless marriages end in divorce. Couples pretend to be happy, withholding the fact that their marriages have been reduced to partnerships for the sake of maintaining convenience and their image. At the same time, there are marriages that still exist, possibly because love remains the focal point. These different perspectives have created challenges for both sexes that have left many with questions and fears! What are your thoughts?

Embrace Your Singleness

I am certainly not the first person to admit being single is easy when you desire a committed relationship. This can be particularly difficult around the holidays and witness other couples creating lasting memories together. It's important to consider why God has you in a place of singleness at this time. You may see couples together seemingly enjoying one another; however do we really know what goes on behind closed doors when they are home and no one is around to judge and or scrutinize the relationship. We need to be mindful of what we pray and ask God for. We do not know what tests and trials she may be experiencing to get to the happy place you see.

Being single is not punishment; it's a blessing when you have the proper perspective. In your singleness be intentional about enjoying the freedom, which comes from being without obligation. Use this time to strengthen and shore up yourself as God prepares you for the mate He has for you. This is your opportunity to focus on your education, career, and or traveling with girlfriends. Your single experiences will add to the person God will present to the man He is creating especially for you. Think about the worldly conversations you will be able to have with your future husband and family. Use your single time wisely; think of this time as you planning for your future!!!

Do you like to cook? Can you cook? Take a cooking class. Are you burdened down with bills, debt, and a poor credit score? Start repairing the areas of your life, which require your immediate attention. Are you happy with you are when you look in the mirror; do you like you? Do you enjoy your own company? In your "**ME**antime" it's imperative you get to smile at the reflection in your mirror.

Food for Thought and Your Consideration:

For some we've become accustomed to uncomfortable or compromising relational situations; we are unable to embrace who we are and/or whose we are, regarding our singleness (Reference Psalm 139)! I'd like you to block out every person you know who is in a healthy or unhealthy relationship for a second and ask yourself these three questions:

1.) What is it within me that desires to be with someone else?

_____
_____
_____
_____
_____

2.) Is it my insecurities or inadequacies that make me yearn for a companion?

_____
_____
_____
_____
_____

3.) Do I feel incomplete? If so, what role do I expect someone else to play that will create completeness within me?

_____
_____
_____
_____
_____

Embracing our singleness is truly a matter of embracing ourselves! Many of us struggle with this reality, possibly because we've been conditioned to continually look outside of ourselves. When we can embrace all of who we are, the chances of us exploring the adventure of healthy and sustainable relationships or marriages will hopefully allow us to fully embrace one another!

Women of Strength

I've been made fun of!
I've been laughed at!
I've been used and I've been abused!
I've made mistakes and I've given my best!
I've been vulnerable and I've been hurt!
I've been told lies and I've struggled with accepting truths!
I've been committed to false commitments and I've fought for what was never mine!
I've argued, had fights, and still ended up alone!
I've been in short-term flings and long-term relationships without a ring!
I've been through a lot, but yet and still I am willing to offer more!
I've endured shame, embarrassment, bitterness, and resentment!
I've been held captive by the chains of un-forgiveness, anger, and revenge!
All I've been through has positioned me to become a woman of strength!
I am much more aware of me than I've ever been before!
I am a woman of Strength!

Ladies, I encourage you to take time to ponder and meditate on these questions. Open your heart and answer honestly. The purpose of this activity is to help you realize how strong you are despite what you've endured in your previous relationships. I want you to remember that YOU ARE STILL HERE and YOU ARE STILL STANDING!

She girds herself with strength, and makes her arms strong.
—Proverbs 31:17

1. Describe attributes about you, which make you a Woman of Strength.
2. Describe a time when you had to deal with hurt in a past relationship. What are some of the ways and/or techniques used to overcome and move forward?
3. Do you spend more time thinking about what hurts you or what strengthens you?
4. What challenges have contributed to your personal growth within past years?
5. Name weaknesses you would like to transform into strengths?
6. What are some of the past hurts and pains hindering you from moving forward?
7. What would you change in order to avoid experiencing the same pain?
8. Read the poem again and explain which parts you can or cannot relate to.

Reflect on the answers to these questions remind yourself you are still here and in the process of moving forward! You are under construction!

The Chains Have Been Broken (Part 1)

It is my firm belief our first encounter with love take place through our parents or guardians. If love and nurturing occurred during crucial developmental stages by those charged with parental authority and care. This is the love we will display. When that love departs there due to separation, or death, the chains of abandonment and fear set in.

Chains with the links of abandonment and fear leave collateral damage and more links of insecurity and distrust. These links bind, thread and knit our perceptions leaving more vulnerable and ripe to experience a false sense love, ripe for inauthentic relationships, and manipulation. Chains of being misunderstood and fear of exposing our authentic selves to others come into fruition.

Relationships often become increasingly difficult to maintain because of past hurts, fears, pains, and chains! To experience the various dimensions of love, one must be willing to not only seek out a healthy and caring love, but also be willing to break our own chains to become vulnerable to trust and love again.

You have the power to break your own chains and love whomever you choose, in spite of the pain from your pass.

I Refuse! (Part I)

We are living in challenging, difficult times; whether health, finances, relational, or an unhealthy self-image.

The images of society's success
are impacting our conscious and shifting our focus toward things.

Money appears to have dominated most conversations and has also become the very reason
most are unable to relate or even interact with one another!
But today, in spite of every trial, test, and situation, you must adopt an I REFUSE Attitude….

-To give up on hope
-To give up on myself
-To give up on others
-To allow the hardships of life keep me down
-To believe God doesn't see me, love me, or abide in me
-To give up on visions and dreams which have been placed in me
-To let society dictate to me what success looks like
-To allow those who've been careless impact my ability to care
-To silence myself because my voice doesn't sound like someone else's
-To let fear intimidate me
-To let the way others view my issues and struggles keep me in chains

I REFUSE to go back I won't back down!
I REFUSE to do anything that doesn't produce life.
I REFUSE!!

FEAR interfere with what you have for me!!!!

The Chains Have Been Broken (Part 2)

It took a long time to heal from that past pain.
That is something that I would not allow myself to feel, taste, or smell ever again!
Oh! I am adamant about not trying love again.
The way I was hurt?
I can't ever see myself giving love another chance to enter in.

I'm not gonna front.

The desire to be IN LOVE remains,
but the fear and potential for pain and heartache outweighs me.

Did I really heal from my past hurt?
Am I quietly suffering because my WALL is up?
Am I allowing FEAR to limit the possibilities and the life God has for me?

Wait a minute . . . I feel a pinch, a nudge in my spirit. I can hear a still small voice:

You are fearfully and wonderfully made!
Let me show you what being in love feels like, smells like, and tastes like.

Start with me first.

Then will you allow love to enter in
because of your relationship with me.
You oh God will guide me, the wall of fear, pain, and heartache are distant, and You are near...

So starting today, I will NOT, I REFUSE to let FEAR interfere with what You have for me!!!!

Bumped Back to Start! "SORRY!"

Growing up one of my favorite board games was "Sorry." To this day generations still enjoy a good game of "Sorry." My friends and I would get a kick out of bumping each other's pawns back to "Start" before making it to the safety zone or home. When one of us bumped another person's pawn back to the start, we would do a celebratory "Sorry" dance to tease our opponents.

The objective is to be the first player to get all four of their color pawns from their start location to their "home" space. The pawns are normally moved in a clockwise direction, but can be moved backward if directed. Movement of pawns are directed by the drawing of a card.

When a player draws a "Sorry" card from the deck, that player has the authority to move his or her pawn from its starting point and bump an opponent's pawn back, taking that player's place while providing an apologetic "Sorry!"

Sometimes life plays out similar to the objective of this board game. You will go through situations that will frustrate you to the point of not knowing where to turn. People will come into your life and hurt you—sometimes intentionally. There will be times when a door will close on a love relationship, a friendship, and/or a career, even after investing your time and energy. The response you will hear is "I'm sorry I stepped out on our relationship" or "I'm *sorry* for hurting you." When your boss tells you are losing your job because they are re-aligning the company, you will hear "I apologize" or "I'm sorry this had to happen to you before the holiday season."

Situations like these bump you back to start, back to the beginning. They put you in a place where you have to start over and leave you feeling frustrated and unsure of what to do! There will be many instances in our lives we cannot control; however, we must ask ourselves what lessons are we learning from these painful circumstances. When a shift occurs in our lives, we move from one location to another, the question is, am I going in the right direction.

Change and starting over can be difficult to accept. But, there is a blessing in going back to start and getting bumped from your spot on the game board of life. For example, J.K. Rowling always dreamed of becoming a writer. She had a nine-to-five job as a secretary, but was fired for spending too much time on the job talking and dreaming about becoming a writer. Look at her now! The author of the "Harry Potter" series, which is tremendously successful!

You have the power to move the bump back to start. Your bump may be a dead relationship, job termination, the loss of a loved one, or a friend who walked away. Use it as an opportunity!!!! You have two choices in life. You can go back to Start and reshuffle the deck, rearrange some things and then move full-steam ahead, or you can go back to Start and stay stuck. Which will you choose?

I Have A Dream...

That one-day, love for God and one another will be the focus of all humanity
That one day, forgiveness won't be forgotten when feelings of hurt, abandonment, resentment, bitterness, and anger block our memory.

That one day, the past will no longer impact our decisions to take advantage of the divine present moments which usher us into hopeful futures.
That one-day, understanding and compassion will kill judgment.
That one-day, titles will be meaningless and no longer separate us.
That one day, we will awaken to the Spirit of God, which abides in us, and we begin to do what God blew His breath into each of us to do.

I have a dream . . .

Those one-day, material things will no longer have more value than human relationships.
That one-day, we will value one another more in life than after death.
That one-day, we will be able to live in harmony without focusing on flaws, struggles, insecurities, inadequacies, finances, or failures.

I have a dream that one day, I will become my dream because I am my dream.

Inspirational Quotes

I would like to share with you some amazing quotes from special people in my life who have inspired me to keep dreaming of better future and a better society of people without judgment based on appearances. These people continue to encourage me to let go and let God, and make incredible contributions for the betterment of people all over the world.

"No one takes care of Number 1 better than Number 1."
—***Andris Thomas***

"Women can be as gentle and soothing as the ocean hitting rocks. Women can be as courageous and powerful as a tsunami, wiping out anything in their way. Like water, life cannot exist with YOU!"
—***Erica Ojada***

"I have the situation; the situation does not have me!"
—***Felicia Adams-Smith***

"Sometimes when I don't get the response I expect from people, I have to remind myself that I help people for God's glory, not validation. People can't bless me; God blesses me. It reminds me that the work I do is for God and not for the validation of people."
—***Miesha Stokely***

You Are Still Here!

God, my God, I yelled for help and you put me together. God, you pulled me out of the grave, gave me another chance at life when I was down-and-out.
—Psalm 30:2 (The Message Bible)

There will be times in our lives when we will mess up.
There will be times in our lives when we will not get it right.
There will be times in our lives when we might think about giving up.
There will be times in our lives when we might just want to walk away from everyone and everything.
There is a possibility that we will make the same mistake over and over and over again and ask ourselves,
"Why can't I get it right?"

Every morning we wake up, God is giving us another chance to get it right! He knows what you will encounter for the day; He knows what is around the corner. He already knows what you are about to do before you do it! He knew your life was not going to be so easy.

In order to use us as living testimonies, God employs life experiences and people to teach us lessons. You cannot beat yourself up, feel defeated, or think that you are unworthy or incapable and continue to apply serious amounts of pressure on yourself because you keep messing up.
Instead of looking at your mistakes, pitfalls, hiccups, and defeats; look at how far you have come! Focus on the progress you have made!
You are not the same person you were before!

You are not what people say about you!
You are not what those negative thoughts in your head say about you!
You are not defeated!
You are a walking testimony!

You are still here!!!

Suppressing the Pains and Living with the Memories

I've learned its extremely challenging to live life to the fullest, dream new dreams, and move on from past agonies of life if you bury hurt while trying to live with the very memories bringing the pain.

I've learned we need to continuously put our best foot forward and attack each day with an attitude of prioritizing! Whether family, work, school, relationships, health, or our vocations, most of us have committed ourselves to taking care of our own individual responsibilities! But even in the midst of tending to our obligations, we have moments when the memories of the past find a way to accompany us along the way. It seems unbearable to live in the face of the very things that could have killed us. As we watch the people we loved leave or pass away, some of us are still holding on to the pain of unanswered questions without closure.

Although it's difficult to live with these day-to-day or moment-by-moment experiences, I do believe it's possible to stop suppressing our struggles and begin countering these thoughts when memories start heading our way! Instead of holding on to things and keeping busy while believing it will somehow miraculously take the pain away, we must allow ourselves to become vulnerable to others who may share the similar feelings with the hopes of easing and releasing the pains that hurt you!

Let's bully our past pains with present healthy and life enhancing affirmations, renewed hopes, and a desire to be better individuals rather than holding on to memories which impact our ability to Live in our Today.

Where Do Broken Hearts Go?

Remember the smash hit *"Where Do Broken Hearts Go?"* by the late, great, Whitney Houston?

"Where do broken hearts go?
Can they find their way home?
Back to the open arms
of a love that's waiting there."

The one who has love waiting for you with open arms is the one who created you and made you. He is the one who designed a plan for you before your parents conceived you. The broken hearted should be able to return home to seek answers to question and heal from wounds; however, unfortunately, most times those who are broken go in the opposite direction, leading to destruction, manipulation, more heartache, bad advice, and difficult lessons learned.

It's important to surround yourself with people you trust and have your best interest at heart.

However, being mindful they can't mend your broken heart, nor do they know the reason you must face the heartache. They are not aware of what God has intended for you to learn through this experience. There have been numerous times when I've gone directly to my friends, in search of answers and comfort when going through something. I'd go to them first instead of communicating with God!

God is fully aware of every situation and encounter you will face. He allows things to happen in your life in order to help you grow. Would you not agree what's best for your broken heart is to take it back to the one who created you? The one who knows how to mend you? Return to the one who knows what is best for you! The Potter wants to put you back together again!!

The question has been proposed: Where do you think broken hearts should go?

Here are some questions to meditate on as you think about broken heartedness:

Is your heart broken?
If so, how did it get broken? (Who broke it?)
Is it still being kept guarded, waiting to be pieced back together?
Did you make it someone else's responsibility to take care of your heart rather than your own?
Have you been more concerned about receiving instead of giving love, and that's what got your heart broken?
Who do you think can heal or fix what has been broken?
If your heart ever becomes healed and ready to love again, what will be different the next time? Now that you've answered these questions, what will you do, and whom will you turn to?

The Familiar vs. The Unfamiliar (Part I)

What is it about us that seek comfort, stability, and security? Is it human nature that yearns for this? I'm not quite sure what it is that causes us to fight for familiarity, but I am starting to see that many of us aren't happy or content with the things that have become too familiar.

There aren't any exceptions in areas of our lives to become discontent about. We are tired of the mate we have, the job we have, the weight we are carrying, and the lack of money we possess. Considering the area(s) of familiarity you focus on most, what will it take to get you out of your boat of comfort and step into the waters of unfamiliar possibility? How long will you continue seeking comfort in the familiar, only to complain about it every day? Do you even recognize that you do this?

What is it about the unfamiliar that scares you? Is it not being in control? Is it resistance to learning something new about you?

The truth of the matter is that we have all arrived where we are as a direct result of entering into the unfamiliar territory mainly because we spent too much time dealing with the familiar! The task is to continue challenging ourselves to pursue what doesn't make us feel comfortable. We should always desire to learn more about ourselves instead of constantly complaining about our situations!

Now are you ready to step out of your comfort zone and explore the benefits that await you? Get out there and meet more of you!!!!

Stop Picking at Your Wounds! Let the Scabs Heal!

Have you ever found yourself going back to situations you knew were not good for you?

Have you ever found yourself revisiting your hurtful past through your thoughts?

Have you ever picked up the phone to reply to a text you know should be erased?

Have you ever been in a place where you entertained the idea of going back because you thought there was a possibility that staying in the past would be better than living in the present?

Have you ever been in a place where you allowed him/her to come to your home just to talk and found yourself in more than just friendly conversation?

Have you ever been in a place where you allowed him/her to walk in and out of your life?

Have you ever allowed yourself to put someone else needs and feelings before your own?

Have you ever kept the door cracked—knowing the door should be shut with a bolted lock—just in case you heard a knock?

Do any of these scenarios describe your past or current situation?

I want to tell you it's important for your healing, your growth, your self-esteem, your confidence, your mental wellbeing, your life, your soul, and your spirit; for YOU to stop picking at your old wounds to allow the scabs heal!

The definition of a scab, taken from the Merriam-Webster Dictionary, is defined as *a hard covering of dried blood that forms over a wound to cover and protect it as it heals*.

The scabs that form over our wounds create memories of what we have been through in our lives. Some scabs are visible and give the impression that whatever caused the wounds must have been very painful. However, the naked eye cannot see the most painful wounds because the inner and the emotional wounds that we as women/men suffer from are not tattooed on our bodies in the form of scabs.

As time passes, most wounds naturally heal from past injuries and life's disappointments. It's imperative for you to allow them to fully heal. You cannot continue going back to the one who hurt you so deeply, even when he/she says they wants to remain friends.

You cannot travel back in time to that abusive relationship because it appears he's/she's "changed." Instead of punching you several times, you begin the shadow box dance."

You cannot allow yourself to entertain conversation, which does not remind or reinforce why you left him/her in the first place, and why you left that so-called friendship.

In order for your scabs to fully heal, move forward without looking back. Don't stop, even for a moment, don't text back, don't even reply back with a simple "hello."

If you allow yourself to keep picking at your scabs, you will continue to bleed with that same hurt and disappointment. Do not let your wounds cause you to keep living in the past! Let your scabs remind you to move forward and use them as you testimony.

You deserve to take time to heal and fully receive God's best for your life! He has wonders to perform in your life if and when you let Him.

I Didn't Know I Needed HEALING!

There was a time when pain was my constant companion and I used it as my excuse to indulge in unhealthy situations, which did nothing to enhance the quality of my life! Losing my dad was a traumatic experience for me. From the age of 15, pain and anger became my best "friends." I used this pain to justify years spent in the streets hustling, I dropped out of school, smoked weed, and drinking to excess!

I recklessly entered into relationships for reasons, which weren't conducive or edifying to either party! I used, misled, and took advantage of women at every opportunity, because my friends "pain and anger" gave me permission! I didn't value or appreciate anyone around me during this time in my life! I journeyed through life aimlessly, seeking attention and approval from people who didn't care about me!

The tears I often shed made little difference because I "didn't know I needed healing!" As I look back over my life, I'm in disbelief at how I engaged others. I hadn't had a true, authentic relationship with anyone. I was in a committed relationship, married to pain and anger. I listened to them more than anyone else and ended up prison!

I didn't recognize I needed healing! I didn't know how angry I was or how I internalized the pain following my dad's passing. The only recurring thought I had at the time was I missed my dad immensely and believed my life would be better had he still been alive.

In this moment of transparency I want to offer a thought to anyone who is reading this:

Recognize your need for inner-emotional and spiritual healing before anger, hurt, resentment, bitterness, sadness, or shame lead you to or keep places which ultimately detour, disrupt, and delay what you were created to do.

I Am God's Masterpiece!

A jewel? A showpiece? A treasure? A gem? A prize? A picture of success? A blockbuster? Who? Me?

Oh no, he can't be talking about me! He must be referring to you! I know he can't be talking about me! I have done so much wrong; I went left when I should've gone right. I don't see anything special when I look in the mirror. People told me my dreams would not come true, they were too big! I was told I wouldn't amount to anything! I focused more on what I did wrong rather than what I did right!

My past failures and thoughts haunted me. Voices in my head told me I would never find love again, among other things: *What makes you think you can write a book? You're not even a good writer. You can't start your own business. Your finances and your credit are jacked up! You will never get that job. You aren't qualified for that position. You lost your job and it's your own fault. You won't get another job that will give you the same or more pay with good benefits. You are never going to lose weight. You eat too many cookies!*

I allowed other people's opinions and thoughts get into my head and adopted these ideas and made them my own! In my mind, I was starting to believe these CRAZY things!

Hold up! Wait a minute!!!!! I am made in God's image!!! God created me, and He loves me so much. I BELIEVE GOD! I am very special in His eyes. Yes, I've made mistakes! I'm not disqualified! My mistakes do not define who I am, and I am not what I used to be. I know my worth. God said to me, *the sooner you see yourself for who you really are, the sooner you can take your reign as my priceless princess with a purpose. You are my masterpiece. You were created in my image and you are indeed a piece of the Master.*

Don't permit other people or the enemy to control your thoughts! Re-evaluate your circles—you might have to let some people go, so you can meet your purpose and be bathed in the blessings God has for you!

A jewel! A showpiece! A treasure! A gem! A prize! A picture of success! A blockbuster! All of the above!

I am God's Masterpiece!!

Haven't You Had Enough?

The question isn't difficult to comprehend! It's simple and direct!

This question challenges us to take a moment to consider various situations we are currently involved in. On the surface we may initially think about everything that isn't going our way and feel as though we've had enough, but I want to challenge you to go deeper within yourself instead of playing it safe by staying on the surface.

To some degree every job and even unemployment have levels of frustration. I'm sure there are annoying friendships, family members and or acquaintances. And I bet you all the 16 bucks I have now (LOL!), that there are some family members and friends—or at least one—whom you are beyond pissed off with!

Circumstances vary for each of us, but I'm willing to bet we've all had enough of these surface situations and want or need an immediate change! I want to address and explore the areas within you, you maybe unaware of or refuse to do anything about.

Haven't you had enough of placing more responsibility on others than you do on yourself?

Haven't you had enough of being bitter because things didn't go your way?

Haven't you had enough of being angry with family or friends because they didn't support you the way you wanted them to?

Haven't you had enough of letting low self-esteem dictate your decision-making?

Come on! Help me out! Fill in the blank for yourself: "I have had enough of _____!" Don't you think it is time to confront yourself instead of always placing the blame on everyone else? How much longer will you hold yourself hostage waiting for someone else to free you?

Hold yourself accountable! Haven't you had enough?

Your Reality vs. Their Perception

How is your reality at this time in your life? Is it one filled with goodness that keeps you smiling and always grateful? Is it one that's become too difficult to come to terms with? Is it one in which you have become so consumed with pleasing others, you're no longer aware of yourself? Or is it all of the above, depending on the occasion?

Our realities tend to shift as we journey through this life. One moment we are aware of ourselves, the next we become so afraid of our circumstances—due to whatever challenges is presented—we are consumed by the perception that others "may have" about what's really going on.

Why do we allow this to happen?

Do yourself a favor and grab a pen and pad and jot down the areas of your reality that have become too difficult to come to terms with. Whether it is your weight; finances; health problems; issues of your past; lack of faith in God or yourself; relationships with family, friends, or a significant other, write it down.

Be mindful that the purpose of this therapeutic exercise isn't to upset or irritate you. It is to re-establish focus and help keep you from dwelling on what others may think or feel about one or all these experiences that have become too difficult for you to confront. If your reality isn't to your liking at this time in your life, you're not alone. We all have those moments when somehow nothing feels right.

Readjust your focus! Embrace and accept your current reality whether good, bad, or both! Dismiss the negative thoughts of how others may perceive you and start caring more about how you see you! Your opinion of yourself is way more important. Let's work toward being OK with our own realities!

The Familiar vs. The Unfamiliar! (Part 2)

Personally I got to a point in my life where I became fed up and tired of everything familiarity. It took an empty relationship, with a side of heartbreak, and a job that was robbing me of my passion and dreams. I wanted God to breathe new life into my world and into my spirit. I wanted to explore a new dimension of me never tapped into. I wanted to taste the essence of what God had for me through unfamiliar territory.

Sometimes we become too comfortable where we are. We want more, but we're scared to step out of the boat into the sea of uncertainty for fear of drowning. "How am I going to pay my mortgage next month?" "What about my medical insurance?" "How can I start over now? I have a family that depends on me." "Why aren't there any more good men/women in this world?"

These thoughts of insecurity trick us into remaining comfortable in unfulfilling life situations. I lived in that mind space for a long time. There were many times in my life when I did step out into the unknown and it was easy for me. However, when it came to my relationships or my job, fear held me hostage. I eventually got to the place where I wanted a different path for my life and I challenged myself to change my situation.

I challenged myself to take control of what I could and pray about those things I couldn't control. I needed to start doing things differently. When my mind, body, and spirit were in sync on newness for my life, my actions followed suit. The unfamiliarity I experienced frightened me a little, and to this day, still has an effect on me. However, through prayer and faith, I learned God has been holding my hand the entire time. He has not and will not leave me, and He will do the same for you. The benefits will be bountiful and you will learn more about YOU. Most importantly, you will learn more about the GOD who is with you and within you!

Step out of the boat! Are you ready for something NEW?

What Is the Last Thing God Said to YOU? (Part 1)

Whether you turn to the right or to the left, your ears will hear a voice behind you, saying, "This is the way; walk in it."
—Isaiah 30:21 (NIV)

While writing this empowerment book, my friend and co-author often had many deep conversations about faith, love, relationships, careers, and many other aspects of life. We continue to have these discussions with each other. They are a tremendous part of the workshops we facilitate around the country.

One evening after one of our meetings, I was expressing to him some of the challenges I had been facing at the company I was working for. At the time, I knew that God was speaking to me about stepping out on faith and making changes in my life according to the vision He had poured into my heart. However, I wasn't sure if I was hearing God's voice or mine. My friend asked, *"What is the last thing that you heard from God?"* Then he asked the same question in a different form: *"When is the last time you heard from God?"* I thought to myself, well, I am in seminary (every day I am reading God's word and books about him). I'm also in prayer every morning. I have my daily devotions, and I attend weekly bible study. So I know God is leading, directing, and speaking to me; however, the question was right on point!

I answered him saying, *"I can't really pinpoint the last thing that God said to me."* Because I was so busy being busy with my busy life. I could not here God's voice clearly. God had been using different people to call me into a place of stillness, but I wasn't listening. I was distracted. I had many encounters with special people in my life that always told me, *"Whitney, you need to be still and listen to what God is trying to speak to you."* I would always agree with them, but never stopped moving. These people were absolutely right. The intimate conversation I had with my co-author resonated with my spirit this particular evening, and it was then I finally heard God telling me he needed me to be still.

We can become so busy in our lives that we develop static in our conversations with God, which can make it difficult to decipher between His words and our own. If you are a person who wants to follow the steps God has for you, make the right decisions about your relationships, step out into a new career, and look for answers from God directly. Not only do you have to pray, fast, and read His word, but also sometimes you just have to be still. Making room for stillness is a priority. You'll be amazed at how many positive realities are birthed from moments of stillness. Your vision will become less cloudy. God's voice will become clearer. You will realize what's effective or ineffective in your life, and you will rediscover dreams and goals you've allowed to die; now may need to be resurrected. Most importantly, you will learn more and more about YOU!

God speaks to us in many different ways. He may use people, reading, music, a dream, or a whisper in your ear, which will resonate in your heart and mind. Discovering the voice of God and recognizing how He speaks to you is essential for self-development. When you know God's voice, you can't be confused when people try and tell you what you are "supposed to be doing" with your life or what God "told them" to tell you. When you are sure what God is speaking into your life, no man or woman can tell you anything different.

Are you ready to walk into what God has for you and HIS will for your life? Aren't you tired of making the same mistakes over and over again? When is the last time you heard God speak to you?

Take some time to answer a few questions:

1. Do you remember the last time God spoke to you? If so, what is the last thing He said?
2. What is currently on your plate that you can remove?
3. What are some things that might prohibit you from having alone time with God?
4. Is keeping busy your way of coping with your feelings? If so, explain why.

People Think They Know, but They Have No Clue!

I was on my way out of church one day when someone asked me, "You quit the choir, too?" I was really caught off guard. The person asked the question is in the "ministry."

Let me give you a little background on why this person made this assumption. I was the leader/president of the young adult (ages 18-40) ministry at my church for three years, the district director of the young adults for the churches of Westchester County for two years, and also a member of my church's young adult choir for 11 years.

There was a time during the three years I was ready to give up the position as the president of the young adult ministry because I did not know how to handle the stress and struggle when it I believed people wanting to take control and didn't understanding I had family, a 9-5, and other responsibilities to attend to. I was encouraged to continue in the position because it was not God telling me to go, it was me. I was the one telling myself to go because I didn't want to deal with the trials and tribulations that came with holding the position.

I decided to stay in the position because I recognized—with the help of others and prayer— it was the enemy trying to take me off course, but God wasn't through using me in this particular position. There was more He needed me to do. However, toward the end of the third year of my presidency, I started noticing a shift in the atmosphere.

My motivation in ministry started to change. I could feel God pulling me into a different dimension of ministry and life. I developed a desire to focus on women, transforming them into what God wants them to be. I wanted to create events for the community that could take place outside the four walls of church to encourage and bring more women to Christ. I started to write books to uplift people. I was certain during the third year of my presidency God was calling me out of that position so He could begin training and transforming my mind. He needed me to spend some quiet time with Him and deepen my relationship with Him, among other things. I knew my time was up! I have always been one who believes when your time is up and God is calling you to move, you need to take the steps to move accordingly.

I was not going to allow myself to stay in a position I would no longer be effective in. I never left my choir; I was took time to get my schedule. It became hectic juggling school, my demanding job, and my son, who is my first priority. My first book was published during that time which opened the door for multiple speaking engagements.

The question about the choir took me by surprise, initially to the point of laughter. But as I made my way outside, I wanted to go back to confront her! That did not happen. I just ministered to myself and realized some important things helped me and may help you if ever you have an encounter or experience a similar situation.

1. Do not allow people to change your decision when you know it was the right one for you.
2. Know when the time is right to step out of a position that God is calling you out of.
3. Understand distractions come in all forms to take you off the destined track God has for you.
4. People are always going to assume that they know your story.

5. Know that people will have their own opinions. Whether or not their opinion matters should depend on who they are.
6. Don't waste your thoughts, time, and energy feeding into their negativity.
7. People do not have to understand your movements.
8. Remember to be obedient to your spirit and instinct.

As long as you are comfortable with the decisions you make in life and you have a sense of peace in your spirit, keep moving. Remembering to carefully step over the many distractions and roadblocks life will put in front in your path!

Learning How to Live with the Judgment

I am starting to believe life takes on new meaning when you allow yourself to live with judgment! I mean, really! How many of us accept/believe the judgment others have placed on us? People close to us have called some of us all types of names. We've received unwanted glares and comments from people who don't even know us; but simply believe something they've heard about us!

Isn't it peculiar how we make mistakes doing things we know we shouldn't do and continue to do them, yet we find ways to place judgment on others? What is our problem? Has no one ever brought this to our attention? How many times a day do you judge someone? Be honest! You've never thought about it, have you?

I can assure you if we make a conscious effort to be mindful of the moments we get caught throwing stones, we may be able to lessen the vicious, destructive cycle of judgment. I suggest starting there as opposed to telling someone else not to be judgmental! But, since this conversation is about learning how to live with the judgment, I will direct the attention to those who want to learn how to live with it rather than lose their sense of identity because of it.

Here we go:

1st: Write down a list of things that you like, love, and dislike about yourself.

2nd: Examine what you have written down and ask yourself: Can I accept what I see and begin to work on the parts of myself that I deem necessary to change?

3rd: Accept all of the things that you have written down!

Honest self-reflection is one of the healthiest things that will assist us when living with judgment. News flash family: we will be judged until the day we die and even after we are put in the ground, so there should come a time when we accept judgment and not allow it to have an impact on our ability to thrive!

I can say my moments of mental, emotional, and spiritual freedom came to me when I accepted ALL of me in spite of others' assessments. Today I accept I cannot always cross all of my t's or dot all of my i's, and I will no longer allow ridicule, judgment, and high expectations to hinder my ability to live!!

Is this an excuse to remain unhealthy or destructive, or as church folks would say, sinful? Not at all! There just comes a time when we have to draw a line in the sand and say, "I will live with all of me," and no longer live in this delusional world of fear and self-deception for the benefit of others. Live with it! I assure you authentic people will gravitate toward you and your ability to live with the beast called Judgment!

What Was the Last Thing God Said to YOU? (Part 2)

Let's begin with this question: **Do you believe in God?**

Before engaging the title for this meditation, we must first acknowledge a belief in God! If your answer is yes, the next question is: **Do you believe God?**

There is a significant difference in these questions. There's having a belief in God, and there's the act of believing! Once again, before we attempt to honestly answer the question of this meditation, we must take into consideration this "believe vs. believing" process as it pertains to you and God!

When I was younger I used to look up in the sky and believe that something greater existed, but couldn't articulate because it was just too vast for my words to express. As I've matured, I have come to my own conclusion I not only believe in God, but I now believe God!

Some of us may or may not believe in God. We've all have experienced challenges in life which may have caused trauma, our spiritually in question, and confusion about God's very existence in our lives and those we love or loved. So as we consider this reality that many have lived with, it is very important to be mindful that some people may only believe *in* a god, and others may not have heard about *believing* God.

In order for you to believe God, it means you must be in relationship with Him. It also means that at one time or another, God has spoken to you! Before you read any more of this, take a moment to ponder what has been written so far:

- When was the last time I heard from God?
- Do I believe in God?
- Do I believe God?
- What is my relationship with God?

Now do yourself a favor and get a pen, pad, or pull out your smartphone and use the memo pad and jot down the last thing you believe, felt, or think God has spoken to you!

When God speaks to us it confirms He is in relationship with us! It's evidence we have passed the "believing in God" phase and entered into the "believing God" phase! I would like to imagine that if or since God spoke to you, He must not only love you and find favor in you, but He must trust you with whatever it is that He spoken to you!

Now once again, what was the thing God said to you?

Pause...Hit the Reset Button.

According to the online Miriam Webster Dictionary, the word "pause" means *"a temporary stop: a period of time in which something is stopped before it is started."*

So many people go through life without taking a pause and end up repeating the same mistakes over and over again. I was in deep reflection one day about the people I've allowed to enter my life. I wasn't always as careful as I should have been, largely because I always saw the good in people, even when they weren't good to me.

When it came to dating, I noticed I was repeating a lot of my past behaviors, but most importantly, I was permitting those I dated or just hung out with to handle me the way they wanted. They often took advantage of my good heart. My girlfriend said to me, "It's never too late to hit the Reset button." I replied, "Pause. You are absolutely right!"

I was so tired of always ending up in the same place, so I had no choice but to say it: PAUSE! This cycle had to stop, and it had to start with me! Just like I had to do, you have to pause and hit the Reset button. Every morning you wake up is another chance for new beginnings, a new day you can use to change your atmosphere and open yourself up to receive NEW beginnings and to do things differently.

I no longer allow people to handle me their way. Why? I realized I was doing way too much adding and depositing, while others were merely subtracting and making withdrawals from my life.

Do you need to hit the rest button to change a situation you're in?

Are there people in your life that you need to put on pause?

If you answered yes to one or both of these questions, you know what you need to do!

"What Is It About Them Doors?" (Part 1)

Sit with this question for a second!

The church doors are sometimes the first and last doors that many have entered. What is happening in people's lives when they think of walking through those doors? Why have so many walked in and, in some cases, out of those doors? What's happening inside and what is keeping us there?

Will we encounter God only when we go through the church doors?

Is it the beauty of God, or possibly the hiding space for unaddressed issues, which keeps us coming through these doors?

Stay tuned and empowered, as we are about to explore what is happening behind the doors of the church!

Does God have another dream for the Church? I believe so!

One of Six...

Most women, if not all, have at one point or another been one of many. I am one of them. I was one of six! You and I know this is not what God designed for us. It took me more than 10 years to finally take my shades off and see what I had allowed myself to be a part of. I allowed my friendship, my spirit, my prayer life, and my body to be chained and connected to someone else's stuff, issues, and mess.

So many women are blinded by man's outer appearance, his spirituality, his friendship, his church life, his conversation, his ability to "minister", and the way he presents himself. Initially, we believe he is genuine and true, only to find out he is a pretender.

I was that woman. A friendship and a bond that had developed over years had "blossomed" into a "relationship" in which I was committed to us, and he was committed to himself. I had no doubt in my mind that this is whom God had for me. He was my best friend. We prayed and fasted together, trusted each other with our secrets, and leaned on each other for Godly advice. We made it our business to spend quality time together and attend each other's family events. We encouraged each other through the good and bad times. But all the while, what he gave me; he was also giving the other *six*.

It wasn't entirely his fault. The signs presented themselves numerous times. My spirit told me it was time to go and I wasn't getting what I deserved. When I tried to leave, I allowed him to manipulate me with his cunning and spiritual attributes. I allowed myself to stay in a relationship that did not provide God's best for me.

So what happened? One of the six became pregnant, I was a wreck, and his hands were around my neck—right in front of her— and he denied having anything to do with me. Of course he had commitment issues; he was only committed to himself! But because I was so hardheaded, this is what it took to get me to really understand.

Sometimes when we are vulnerable, not knowing who we are and or whose we are, we will settle for less than what God has for us and walk right pass our blessings. We lose sight of what God is trying to reveal to us. When we are unaware of the power God has equipped us with, we end up in these types of situations. When we don't know our value, we place our trust into people, instead of God, and we lose a part of ourselves.

I got tired of being manipulated. I wanted more. I was tired of patching up holes on the boat. The more I kept trying to convince him of my worth and value and why he should be fully committed to me, the more I kept hearing the same excuses. I was tired of being lied to. I was drained and depleted.

After all I had already been through with this man, it took that encounter to wake me up. I made up in my mind and knew I deserved better. This was not in God's plan for me! In order for Me to do better, I had to start being better. I promised myself that I would not settle for less than God's best in all areas of my life. I will continue to work on transforming myself into the woman who God wants me to be and wait on Him to bring the husband He has already designed for me. I'm under construction. He's preparing for my King.

When Being Vulnerable and Exposed Hurts!

Allowing yourself to become vulnerable again after life deals you a crushing blow is challenging. The feelings we had before and after troubling events can seem too overwhelming to bare. We might start to believe keeping our emotions bottled up is normal.

We subconsciously keep emotional issues to ourselves, believing the problems will either get better or eventually go away. But, we fail to realize that as old situations are lingering, new circumstances are constantly arising. In addition to unknowingly carrying unhealthy perceptions and unrealistic expectations, we become engulfed in ourselves and at times insensitive to others, which makes being vulnerable and exposing our true feelings seem almost impossible.

As we consider this process as it evolves over a period of time, we eventually arrive at a point where we're able to fathom the idea of sharing what is actually happening to us. This, of course, will leave us vulnerable and exposed because we have committed to doing something we have resisted for so long. It may be hurtful if the person(s) you shared your true feelings with doesn't respond to you in a manner that makes you feel comfortable about sharing. They may not understand you. They might judge you, and you may be left alone after taking the risk to share your feelings. You may regret allowing yourself to take a chance on vulnerability.

But you know what? Your vulnerability and exposure isn't for the person you are sharing your past or present moments with; it's for you! It may empower others to become vulnerable and exposed with whomever they choose, but your moments of sharing are primarily for your own growth, emotional, and spiritual stability. Yes, being vulnerable and exposed hurts, but your sanity depends on it! We can't afford to let life have such an impact that it renders us unstable. Be vulnerable and exposed. Be transparent. Be open. Be honest and truthful.

Don't be apprehensive about sharing your feelings when it pertains to your life and the lives of others, no matter how painful that is! Being vulnerable and exposed hurts, but it also HEALS!!

"What Is It About Them Doors?" (Part 2)

Have you given this question any thought? Does it make you uncomfortable to think about it?

Or is joy and peace dancing around your mind at the very thought of this question?

What is it about the doors of the church? What comes to mind when you hear the word *church*? God? Jesus? Love? Forgiveness? Peace? Happiness? The Holy Spirit or Holy Ghost? Change? Heaven and riches? Or does your mind go to the opposite side: Hypocrites? Frauds? Liars? Pimps? Controlling institution? Judgers? Loveless people? People who don't practice what they preach? Plain old phoniness? Or is it all of the above? Neither side is wrong or right; they are simply your thoughts, and that is fine!

Could it be our perceptions of how we feel the church should be shape? How we characterize what we see once we enter those doors? Could it be others' opinions have shaped the language we use to articulate what happens behind the doors of the church? Or has it been our encounter within the church that has us leaning toward the good side or the not-so-good side of the church?

Should we discourage others who may not know what it is like inside the church from walking through those doors because of the not-so-good experiences we may have had? No matter how rich or poor people are, the church has been and continues to be a place of escape as well as a place of hope for those who can't escape their reality.

What is it about them doors?

I would like for someone to talk to me about these questions!

Speak Life! (Part 1)

The tongue has the power of life and death, and those who love it will eat its fruit.

—Proverbs 18:21

Do you believe your life is precious? Are you aware that if you waste time not living your life, letting life live for you, these are days you can never get back? Are you aware that what you think and what you speak can create your atmosphere?

Life can lead us to question ourselves and ask, "How did I end up here?" If you are breathing today, you will experience the ups and downs life has to offer, if you haven't already. However, what's most important is what you speak into your life's situation and circumstances.

After dealing with a lot of hurt, pain, sadness, and disappointment in my life, there was a time when I would speak negatively about my life. I didn't allow myself to speak hope into my future. When I was speaking of hopelessness, situations in my life did not turn around for the better. I would say things like, "I am broken"; "I don't believe things will change"; "I have been defeated"; or "I am never going to love again." Once I recognized what I was doing to myself, I started to change the way I spoke. Friends, prayer, and inspirational reading helped me make this transition. The more my words and thoughts changed, the more my atmosphere began to shift.

Sistas, I am here to urge you to speak life into your own life!!!! Know that the tongue has power and strength to change the atmosphere, create great opportunities for you, and heal you! Be good to yourself and know that your life is too precious to let it slip away. Speak life and watch what God does.

When was the last time you spoke life into yourself?

When was the last time you spoke life into your situations?

How So You Benefit by Being in Competition with Me?

I was required to take a "preaching" class to fulfill requirements for my degree. Everyone in the class was encouraged to preach a sermon. The purpose of the course was to help us sharpen our skills, learn different preaching styles, and to assist with the preparation process. For my sermon, I was led to preach 1 Samuel, Chapter 1, verses 1–20.

As I prepared for my sermon, several aspects of this scripture's story captured my attention, specifically the relationship between Penniah and Hannah. In 1 Samuel, God blessed Penniah with 10 sons. However, He chose to close Hannah's womb, and Penniah teased Hannah because of her condition. For years she tormented and bullied Hannah, but Hannah never retaliated. Instead she chose to take her troubles to God in the form of prayer.

This story reminded me of how some women govern themselves today. It reminds me of the experiences I have faced through interactions with other women. Similar to Penniah, there are many women whose character unfortunately keeps them from empowering their fellow sisters.

Why is this? Why is it so hard for women to be kind and encourage one another to do and be better? Why are some women threatened by another woman's beauty? How does it benefit you being in competition with another woman? You don't! The only thing it does for you is reminding you of how you really feel about yourself!

We don't have time to be in competition with one another! If anything, we need to be there for one another, providing encouragement and support. As women, our lives are filled with so many challenges. We coordinate going to school, going to church, being wives and mothers, managing our careers—which may mean working more than one job—and a host of other things we don't have hands enough to juggle, but we still find a way to make it all happen!

Instead of Penniah tormenting Hannah, she should have said, "Hey girl, I know this thing is really bothering you. I would probably have a heavy heart, too, if God didn't bless me with my 10 sons. But just like God did it for me, He can do it for you."

It's OK for you to say, "Girl you are wearing those shoes!" or "Girl let me help you with your resume so you can get out of this dead-end gig." It's OK to ask, "Sis, where did you get that dress?" or "Can you give me some tips on how you acquired that position?" or "How did you handle being single before God blessed you with your husband?" It's OK!

It is so important for us as women to look out for one another! Penniah was not encouraging; however, because Hannah went straight to God with her troubles instead of firing back, He opened her womb and she received her blessings. What God has for you is for you! So there is no reason you should ever be threatened by another woman's blessings or situation. Let's come together as one and get it together! If we put our strengths together, we are forces to be reckoned with! When will you realize there is no benefit in being in competition with her?

Speak Life! (Part 2)

Have you ever even considered speaking life before?

What does speaking life even mean to you?

Do you want to keep living? How has life been treating you lately?

Life can be inconsistent at times, making it difficult for you to speak anything positive or hopeful into the universe.

Life can be so painful and overwhelming, it can silence you in such a way that uttering any words can just add more pain.

Life can be so confusing at times it will leave you struggling to establish direction and focus.

Life can be whatever we want it to be when we tap into the powerful spirit that dwells within.

Are you willing to tap into that spirit so you can begin speaking life over your life and the lives of those around you?

Breaking Boxing Match News: Me vs. Myself!

According to sources, "Me" has no chance in this world against "Myself" due to previous victories and knockouts against Myself and other opponents.

However, others saw Me in the training facility throwing sharp jabs and landing several left killer hooks in the ring with a trainer. This was a sight no one had ever seen before. Their eyes were glued on her in amazement in the training facility as she was preparing for her third fight with her contender—Myself. Over the years, Me and Myself developed an internal war that was invisible to the naked eye, and kept secret from their family, friends, the boxing industry, and the media.

During the last two press conferences before the matches, the fighters lashed out with massive intensity toward each other with negative allegations and innuendos. This is pretty typical of professional boxers before they enter the ring, so both fighters' supporters held them back and advised them to "save it for ring!"

It was the night of the big fight. Both boxers were running and jumping in place in their respective corners, ready for the fight to start. This is the night they both had been waiting for. The bell went off and round one was underway. The opponents shifted from place to place. Then Myself threw the first blow. Me swung her head and avoided it. Me then threw a punch into Myself's body. Myself replied aloud, "That was weak. It didn't even hurt. That's all you got?"

The rounds came and went. Myself won the majority of the rounds. Me won only three. It was now time for Round 12, the final round. The audience noticed both contenders were growing weary and ready for the fight to be over. Myself was surprised that Me lasted so long, especially knowing she had knocked her out before. Myself started using more hateful tactics similar to what she had done in previous fights. It worked on Me back then, but would it work this time?

As the round progressed, Myself grabbed Me and whispered in her ear, "Remember what they used to say about you. You're weak. You don't have what it takes to be successful" as she threw Me to the ground. Me got up and threw a left hook, to which Myself responded with an upper cut. Me fell down and the referee started counting, one, two, three . . . Me managed to get up and regain her stance. Myself started yelling, "You always fail before you even try! You don't believe in yourself!"

Everything Myself taunted Me with brought back painful memories of what her family and so-called friends said about her. Me's jabs starting landing consistently on target. Teardrops ran down her bloodshot-red face. As myself came back with a left hook, she said to Me, "You are so insecure, you don't even know who you are. Why are you here? You can't win this fight!" Me started going even harder, but Myself's ranting's distracted her, and she was knocked flat on her face. The referee started counting again, one, two, three, four, five . . . all the way to ten. Me never got back up.

Myself had regained her title, started jumping around and shouting. Her team came and picked her up in a celebratory dance. Me was so embarrassed…she stayed down. The shame of letting Myself distract her and win was too much. As she lay there, Me realized that all this time she always had the power to win. But she allowed herself to get in her own way.

How many times are you going to let your insecurities get in the way of you moving forward?

How many times have you talked yourself out of your goals and dreams?

When are you going to deal with and recover from your past so that you can go forward into your future?

ABOUT THE AUTHORS ...

Whitney D. Smith

Circumstances don't always bind us . . . sometimes they inspire us.

When author Whitney Smith stopped to hear the voice of the Lord, nothing else mattered. Smith, a natural leader who strives to enhance lives and promote positivity through Christ, self-awareness, definition of self, and self-efficacy, has dedicated her life to Christian-servitude.

Born in New Rochelle, New York to an educator Dr. Brenda Smith and a minister Rev. Dr. Gregory Smith, Whitney Smith was well grounded in intellectual matters and Christian morals prior to her attaining a Bachelor's of Mass Communication degree from Lincoln University in Oxford, PA (1999). Whitney's credentials led her to attain a position with broadcast and telecommunications giant, Verizon Communications. There Whitney served in several capacities, but it was her excellence in management sales that soon led her to gain managerial positions at two of the Big Four banking corporations, JP Morgan Chase Bank and Wells Fargo and Company, respectively.

As a thriving professional in Corporate America, and now a MBA graduate of Long Island University, Whitney enjoyed the lifestyle she had acquired from her business affiliations. However, Whitney could not deny the Lord's calling on her life. As a teenager, Whitney turned to narcotics and engaged in violent behavior from what she felt would relieve her of the emotional anguish of rape and soothe the pleasure of depraved friendships; and now as an overcomer, Whitney had to fulfill the purpose God had for her life. Whitney stepped down from Corporate America and stepped out on faith towards God's plan.

Surrendering to God's word, Whitney experienced emancipatory transformation whereas the Holy Spirit led her to enroll in New York Theological Seminary, to attain a Masters of Divinity. Ms. Smith is accepting her calling and using the skills she acquired in her Corporate America experience to win lives for Christ, with a primary focus on Women Empowerment. Moreover, Whitney has been frequently applauded for her candid conversations and insightful relationships with younger generations.

This spirit-led entrepreneur, author, public speaker, member of the Zeta Nu Omega Chapter of Alpha Kappa Alpha Sorority, Incorporated, member of the African-American Coalition of Westchester, and member of Greater Centennial African Methodist Episcopal Zion Church in Mount Vernon, NY is ready, aimed, and equipped to create avenues through various media channels and sources that will inspire, challenge, and transform lives into what God has created them to be.

Whitney has served as a guest speaker and workshop facilitator at various venues presenting her works, *Whit's Notes: The College Cheat Sheet* and her co-authored book *Meeting the Authentic You*. Her meditation ministry *Monday Morning Glory,* is purposed to connect believers to spiritual disciplinary initiatives and reflect on God's destiny for our lives.

She the proud mother of a 13-year old honor student and athlete, Avery Turton.

Whit's wit, willingness, and wisdom is her way to His worth.

For more information about Whitney, workshops and products, I invite you to visit-

www.whitneydsmith.com

Dwayne Graham

"I overcame so I can help others overcome"

These words come from a man that many may know but quite few understand. Dwayne was born in Harlem to Laura n Donald Graham in 1975.

From the day Dwayne was conceived, he was forced to go through many trails n tribulations.

By the age of 15, Dwayne lost his father to HIV. Depressed and upset, Dwayne turned to the streets and began to hustle. Drinking and selling drugs became the norm for him.

As one would assume this type of life style would ultimately lead to jail or death, and in most cases, that's true.

Dwayne was arrested and sentenced to 5 years to life at the age of 19. Leaving his 4 brothers and mother behind Dwayne went to prison.

While in prison Dwayne searched for help. Dealing with his fathers death, the guilt of abandoning his mother, and this new life threatening environment, Dwayne was able to find God. Begging for forgiveness and help, Dwayne prayed to remove the taste of alcohol from his tongue, the touch of drugs off his hands, and in return more God in his heart.

"Pain robbed me of my identity"

At the age of 23 Dwayne was released from jail and returned to his family. With a new outlook on life and a supportive mother behind him, Dwayne was able to succeed and enrolled himself into college. But life and God were not through with him.

After being home for only 3 years, Dwayne lost his mother to cancer. Feeling abandoned and alone Dwayne continued to push through and furthermore count on God to guide him.

In the year 2008, when Dwayne was 29, he received a Bachelors degree from Metropolitan College of New York. Dwayne continued to work in the social services field, helping those with mental and medical disabilities become independent and self sufficient in their community. This was part of Dwayne's way of giving back.

"My Divinity kept me when my humanity failed me"

After almost 11 years In the social services field, Dwayne was fired. The reasoning was not understandable but Gods purpose was. Instead of searching for another job, Dwayne went back to school but this time for something different.

Dwayne enrolled into the New York Theological Seminary school. He set out to learn all that he could about God, religion and himself so that he could put it back into the world and create something that would grab the attention of children, adults, and even the non believers.

Starting with a single idea, Dwayne and his friends created a brand, Healthy "r" us. The goal was to connect with everyone through a common need, clothing. T-shirts, hats, and hoodies all carrying the HRU logo. Dwayne and friends decided that it was time to empower those in their community to be more, do more and finally want more.

Workshops, work out groups and counseling sessions. These are all the ways in which Dwayne connects with his community to help encourage them to be the best they can be.

In 2014, Dwayne graduated with a masters degree in divinity. His heart was open, eyes were clear, and his mission was set in stone.

The man referred to in this biography as Dwayne has done more than just survive, he has prevailed. Throughout his entire life God pushed Dwayne in order for him to discover who he really was.

So with all the honor, I don't want to simply introduce Dwayne the man from the story but Dwayne Graham the man ready and willing to show you D'Way.

For more information about Dwayne, workshops and products, I invite you to visit-

www.hru.org

RECEIVED MAR 6 - 2019

2\x